Now I Know

About:

- Counting
- Thinking Skills

Written by: Heddrick McBride

Illustrations: New Way Solutions

Cover: Alex Baranov

ISBN: 1480231908
ISBN-13:978-1480231900

Number 0

0

Zero

Number 1

One Cat

Number 2

Two Soccer Balls

Number 3

Three Elephants

Number 4

Four Footballs

Number 5

Five Apples

Number 6

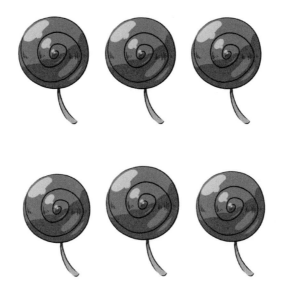

Six Lollipops

Number 7

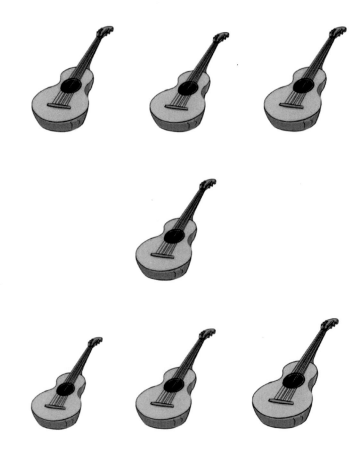

Seven Guitars

Number 8

Eight Airplanes

Number 9

Nine Pumpkins

Number 10

Ten Cheeseburgers

Counting

Count up to 10.

| 1 | 2 | 3 | 4 | 5 | 6 | 7 | 8 | 9 | 10 |

Counting

Count up to 10. Fill in the empty boxes.

1		4	6	8	10

Counting

Count up to 10. Fill in the empty boxes.

How Many Do We Have?

Example: How many frogs do we have?

answer $\underline{3}$

1.How many pizzas do we have?

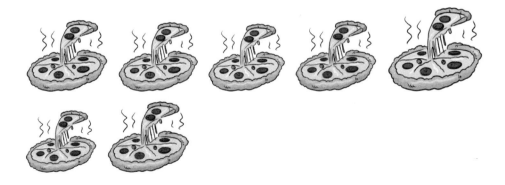

_____

How Many Do We Have?

2. How many drum sets do we have?

_____

3. How many pineapples do we have?

_____

How Many Do We Have?

4. How many broccoli sticks do we have?

_____

5. How many zebras do we have?

_____

How Many Do We Have?

6. How many pairs of ice skates do we have?

_____

7. How many ballerinas do we have?

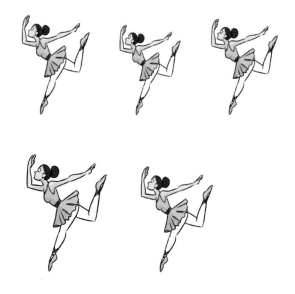

_____

How Many Do We Have?

8. How many bananas do we have?

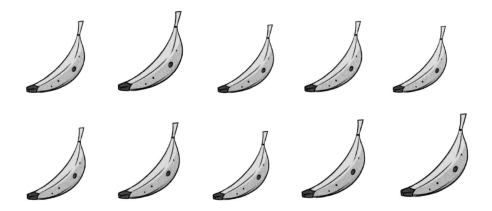

_____

9. How many Skylars do we have?

_____

Things that belong together

Fruits

Animals

Shapes

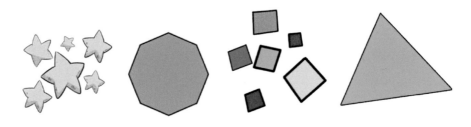

Things that belong together

Instruments

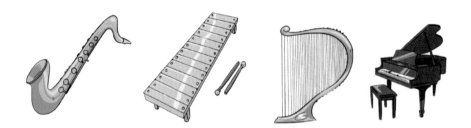

Sports

Vegetables

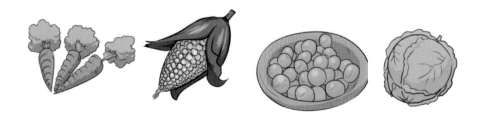

Things that belong together

Bathroom Items

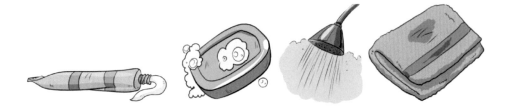

Drinks

Letters

A   X   D   Z

Which object **does not** belong?

Circle the object that **does not** belong.

Which object **does not** belong?

Circle the object that **does not** belong.

Matching

Draw a line from each object to its match.

Matching

Draw a line from each object to its match.

Matching

Draw a line from each object to its match.

Things that go together

Circle two objects **that go** together.

Which one is the Biggest?

Circle the object that is the **biggest**.

Which one is the Biggest?

Circle the object that is the **biggest**.

Which one is the Smallest?

Circle the object that is the **smallest**.

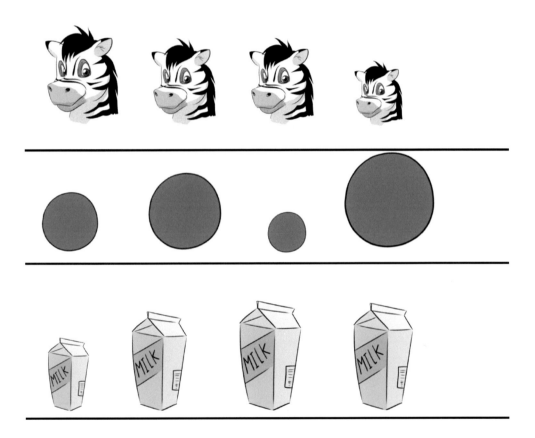

Which one is the Smallest?

Circle the object that is the **smallest**.

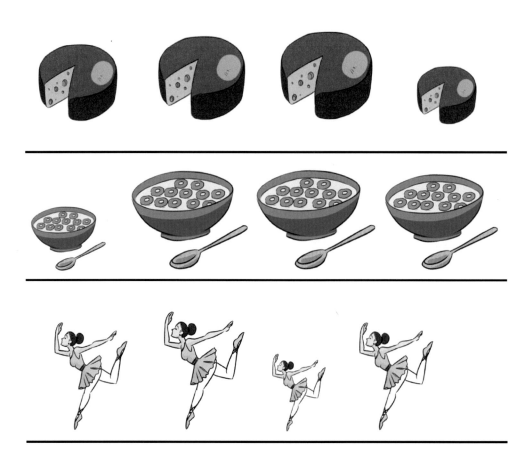

What comes next?

Draw the food that comes next.

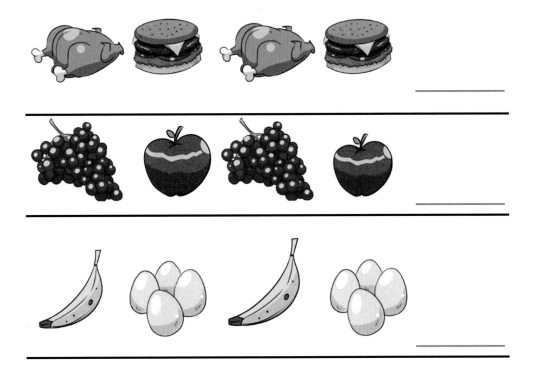

What comes next?

Draw the shape that comes next.

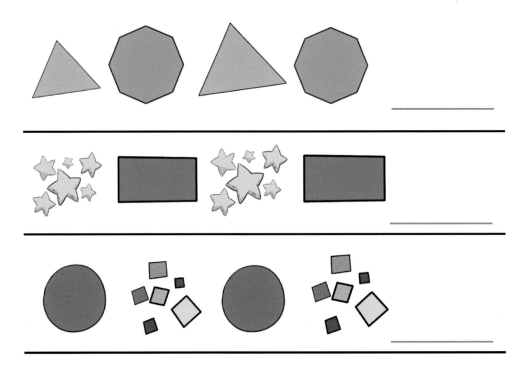

Visit www.mcbridestories.com for more

g Skills

titles.